With Jesus Always

My Mass, Reconciliation, and Prayer Book

William H. Sadlier, Inc.

Nihil Obstat
Reverend James J. Uppena
Censor Deputatus

Imprimatur
✠ Most Reverend Cletus F. O'Donnell
Bishop of Madison
October 23, 1990

The nihil obstat and imprimatur are
official declarations that a book or
pamphlet is free of doctrinal or moral
error. No implication is contained
therein that those who have granted
the nihil obstat and imprimatur agree
with the contents, opinions, or
statements expressed.

Home Office: 9 Pine Street
New York, NY 10005-1002

ISBN: 0-8216-1632-9
    9/9876

Acknowledgements
Excerpts from the English translation of *The
Roman Missal* ©1973, International Committee
on English in the Liturgy, Inc. (ICEL); excerpts
from the English translation of *Rite of Penance*
©1974, ICEL. All rights reserved.

Photo Credits:
Diane J. Ali 55.
Jeffrey Aranita 43.
James Carroll 42, 58, 60.
CROSIERS: Gene Plaisted, OSC 61, 64.
Myrleen Ferguson 33, 53, 54.
Lawrence Migdale 28.
Mark Mittleman 59, 63.
Howard E. Simmons 5, 8, 12, 14 - 15, 16, 17, 18
19, 21, 23, 24, 25, 26.
UNICORN: Betts Anderson 20.
Jim Whitmer 34, 50, 62.

Illustrators:
Adam Gordon, Jim Spence, Maria Cartier

Cover Art:
Grace Kao

Photo Research:
Jim Saylor

Design:
Grace Kao/Kelly Kao

Contents

Ask someone in your family to help you fill in this promise.

I Belong

At Baptism I became a member of the Catholic Church.

I belong to _____
   Parish.

I belong to the _____
   family.

I promise to pray for the whole Church, my parish, my family, and everyone who needs my prayers.

_____
(Your Name)

_____
(Date)

Our Mass Begins
(Introductory Rites)

STAND

A Song

We sing to celebrate that we are
gathered together with
Jesus Christ and one another.

Sign of the Cross

We make the sign of the cross on
ourselves as the priest says:

† In the name of the Father,
    and of the Son,
    and of the Holy Spirit.

We answer:
  Amen.

Greetings

The priest welcomes everyone with these or other words:

The grace of our Lord Jesus Christ and the love of God and the fellowship of the Holy Spirit be with you all.

We answer:
   And also with you.

God Forgives Us — (Penitential Rite)

We praise and ask God to forgive us.

Together we may pray:

I confess to almighty God,
and to you, my brothers and sisters,
that I have sinned through my own fault
in my thoughts and in my words,
in what I have done,
and in what I have failed to do;
and I ask blessed Mary, ever virgin,
and all the angels and saints,
and you, my brothers and sisters,
to pray for me to the Lord our God.

We may repeat after the priest or one of his assistants:

   Lord, have mercy.
   Christ, have mercy.
   Lord, have mercy.

Gloria

We praise God. We say together:

Glory to God in the highest,
    and peace to his people on earth.

Lord God, heavenly King,
almighty God and Father,
    we worship you, we give you thanks,
    we praise you for your glory.

Lord Jesus Christ, only Son of the Father,
Lord God, Lamb of God,
you take away the sin of the world:
    have mercy on us;
you are seated at the right hand
        of the Father:
    receive our prayer.

For you alone are the Holy One,
you alone are the Lord,
you alone are the Most High,
    Jesus Christ, with the Holy Spirit,
    in the glory of God the Father. Amen.

Opening Prayer

**The priest then says a
brief prayer in our name.**

We answer at the end:
    Amen.

Liturgy of the Word

During this part of the Mass we listen to God's word from the Bible. The Bible stories tell us how much God loves and cares for us.

First Reading

Lector:
    The word
        of the Lord.

We answer:
    Thanks be to God.

After the first reading a psalm is read. We say a response that the reader gives us.

Second Reading

Lector:
    The word
        of the Lord.

We answer:
    Thanks be to God.

Alleluia or Gospel Acclamation

As we stand for the reading of the gospel, we join with others in saying or singing Alleluia or another prayer during Lent. The Alleluia is a song of praise to God.

Gospel

In the gospel Jesus speaks to us.

Before reading the gospel the deacon or priest says:
    The Lord be with you.

We answer:
    And also with you.

The deacon or priest says:
    A reading from the holy gospel according to

_____ .
                (Name of Evangelist)

We answer:
    Glory to you, Lord.

At the end of the gospel the deacon or priest says:
    The gospel of the Lord.

We answer:
    Praise to you, Lord Jesus Christ.

SIT

Homily

We listen while the priest helps us to
think about the readings from the Bible.
We call this part of the Mass the homily.

STAND

Profession of Faith

**The Nicene Creed is an ancient way of
saying what we believe.**

We believe in one God,
   the Father, the Almighty,
   maker of heaven and earth,
   of all that is seen and unseen.

We believe in one Lord, Jesus Christ,
   the only Son of God,
   eternally begotten of the Father,
   God from God, Light from Light,
   true God from true God,
   begotten, not made, one in Being
     with the Father,
   Through him all things were made.
   For us men and for our salvation
     he came down from heaven:

by the power of the Holy Spirit
   he was born of the Virgin Mary,
     and became man.

For our sake he was crucified under
    Pontius Pilate;
he suffered, died, and was buried.
On the third day he rose again
    in fulfillment of the Scriptures;
he ascended into heaven
    and is seated
    at the right hand of the Father.
He will come again in glory
    to judge the living and the dead,
    and his kingdom will have no end.

We believe in the Holy Spirit, the Lord,
    the giver of life,
who proceeds from the Father and the Son.
With the Father and the Son he is
    worshiped and glorified.
He has spoken through the Prophets.
We believe in one holy catholic and
    apostolic Church.
We acknowledge one baptism for the
    forgiveness of sins.
We look for the resurrection of the dead,
    and the life of the world to come. Amen.

Another profession of faith,
the Apostles' Creed, is on page 51.

STAND

General Intercessions
(Prayer of the Faithful)

During this prayer we pray for the Church, the Pope, our leaders, our country, our family, our parish, and all those in need.

We usually say after each prayer:
Lord, hear our prayer.

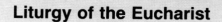

Liturgy of the Eucharist

SIT

The Preparation of the Altar and the Gifts

As a song is sung our gifts of bread and wine are brought to the altar. The priest prays and thanks God for the gift of bread.

We may say:
  Blessed be God for ever.

Then the priest thanks God for the gift of wine.

We may say:
  Blessed be God for ever.

The priest then prays that our gifts, our sacrifice, will be acceptable to God the Father.

We answer:
  May the Lord accept the sacrifice
    at your hands
  for the praise and glory of his name,
  for our good, and the good of
    all his Church.

Prayer over the Gifts

The priest asks God to accept our gifts.
At the end of the prayer we say:
Amen.

The Eucharistic Prayer

We join with the priest to give thanks
and praise to God.

STAND

Preface

The priest begins by praying:
The Lord be with you.

We answer:
And also with you.

The priest prays:
Lift up your hearts.

We answer:
We lift them up to the Lord.

The priest prays:
Let us give thanks to the
Lord our God.

We answer:
It is right to give him
thanks and praise.

At the end of the preface the priest raises his arms and we sing together.

Holy, holy, holy Lord,
   God of power and might.
Heaven and earth are
   full of your glory.
Hosanna in the highest.

Blessed is he who
   comes in the name
   of the Lord.
Hosanna in the highest.

KNEEL

As the priest continues the prayer
we remember the story of Jesus'
Last Supper. The priest recalls what
Jesus did.

The priest takes bread and says:

> Take this, all of you, and eat it:
> this is my body which will be given
> up for you.

The priest shows everyone
the consecrated bread,
which is now the
body of Christ.

Then he takes the cup of wine
and says the words of Jesus:

Take this, all of you, and
    drink from it:
this is the cup of my blood,
the blood of the new and
    everlasting covenant.
It will be shed for you and for all
so that sins may be forgiven.
Do this in memory of me.

The priest shows the cup, which
contains the blood of Christ.

We believe that the bread and wine
are now the body and blood of Christ Himself.

The priest then asks us to proclaim our faith.
We answer with these or other words:

Christ has died,
Christ is risen,
Christ will come again.

The priest and people continue to pray.
Then the priest, raising up both the
plate with the consecrated bread
and the cup, says:

Through him, with him, in him,
in the unity of the Holy Spirit,
all glory and honor is yours,
almighty Father,
for ever and ever.

We answer:
Amen.

19

STAND

Communion Rite
Lord's Prayer

**Together with the priest we pray the
prayer Jesus taught us:**

Our Father, who art in heaven,
hallowed be thy name;
thy kingdom come;
thy will be done on earth
    as it is in heaven.
Give us this day our daily bread;
and forgive us our trespasses
as we forgive those who trespass
    against us;
and lead us not into temptation,
but deliver us from evil.

**The priest says a prayer
and we answer:**

For the kingdom,
    the power and the
    glory are yours,
    now and for ever.

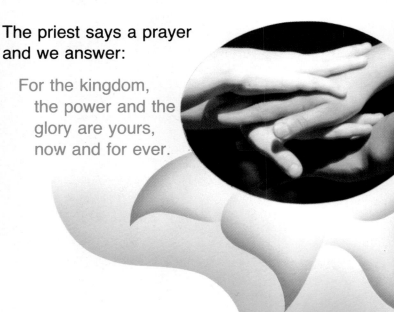

Sign of Peace

The priest prays that Jesus Christ will give us the gift of peace.

We answer:
Amen.

He then says:
The peace of the Lord be with you always.

We answer:
And also with you.

We give a sign of peace, like a handshake or a hug, to those around us.

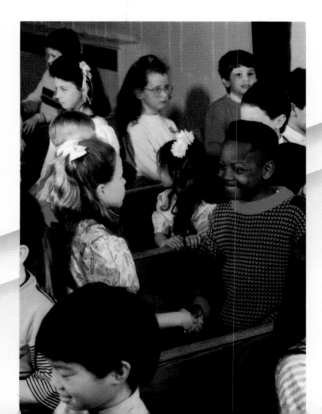

STAND

Breaking of the Bread

**We sing together this prayer
for God's mercy:**

Lamb of God, you take away the sins of
the world:
have mercy on us.
Lamb of God, you take away the sins of
the world:
have mercy on us.
Lamb of God, you take away the sins of
the world:
grant us peace.

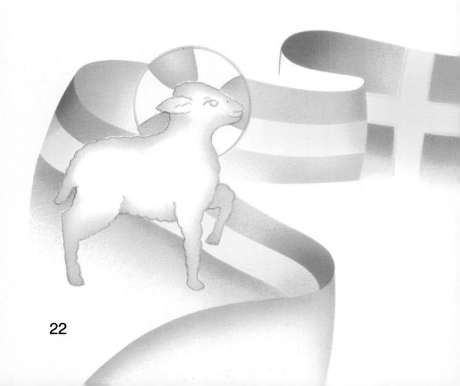

Communion

Now we get ready to receive
Jesus Christ in holy communion.

The priest says:

This is the Lamb of God
who takes away the sins of the world.
Happy are those who are called to his supper.

Together with the priest we pray:

Lord, I am not worthy to receive you,
but only say the word and I shall be healed.

We sing a song as we come forward
to receive communion.

The priest or eucharistic minister places the
host in our hand or on our tongue, saying:
  The body of Christ.

We answer:
  Amen.

If we receive in the hand, we place the
host in our mouth and swallow it.

If we receive on our tongue, we swallow
the host.

If we are receiving from the cup,
the minister says:
>The blood of Christ.

We answer:
>Amen.

Then we take a sip from the cup.

We return to our places, join in the communion
song, and talk quietly with Jesus Christ.
We may also say a favorite prayer.

The priest invites us to pray and
says a brief prayer.

We answer:
>Amen.

STAND

Our Mass Ends
(Concluding Rite)

At the end of the Mass the priest
asks God to bless our whole parish family.

Greeting

The priest prays:
  The Lord be with you.

We answer:
  And also with you.

Blessing

The priest prays:
  May almighty God bless you,
    the Father, and the Son,†
      and the Holy Spirit.

We answer:
  Amen.

Dismissal

The deacon or priest then says:

- Go in the peace of Christ.

                OR

- The Mass is ended, go in peace.

                OR

- Go in peace to love and serve
  the Lord.

We answer:
Thanks be to God.

We sing together a closing hymn.

After we leave the church, we greet the priest and others who celebrated Mass with us.

We carry in our hearts the promises we made at Mass to try to live as disciples of Christ each day during the coming week.

We leave Mass to journey or go forth together to live as Jesus' peacemakers at home, at school, in our neighborhood, and parish.

My First Communion Song

1. Jesus, you come to me
   As Bread to feed me,
   Friend to heal me,
   Light to lead me.
   Welcome, Jesus, welcome.

2. My Jesus, stay with me!
   I want to know you,
   I want to love you, I want
       to serve you
   This day and always.

3. Jesus, I pray to you
   For those who love me,
   Those who teach me,
   Those who care for me!
   Keep them in your heart.

Music for this song can be found on
Sadlier's *With You Always: First Eucharist* Video.

How I Receive Jesus in Communion

If I want to receive the consecrated bread, or host, in the hand, this is what I do:

- Walk to the altar with hands joined.
- Think about Jesus, whom I will receive.
- As my turn comes, I cup my left hand on top of my right hand (or the opposite if you are left-handed).
- When I hear the words "the body of Christ," I answer "Amen."
- After the consecrated bread is placed in my hand, I step to the side. I face the altar and place the consecrated bread in my mouth. I swallow it and return to my seat.

If I receive on my tongue, I swallow the host and return to my seat.

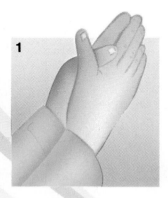

If I am also going to receive from the cup, I swallow the bread, or host, and move to the minister holding the cup.

- When I hear the words "the blood of Christ," I answer "Amen." **3**
- Then I take a sip from the cup.
- I return to my seat and sing the communion song with everyone.
- I spend time just with Jesus. I name all the things for which I want to thank Jesus. Then I name all the things or favors I want to talk to Jesus about.
- I say an after-communion prayer. (See pages 29 or 33.)

Prayers Before Communion

Before receiving the body and blood of Christ in communion we should pause and think of what we are doing. We can say prayers like these:

My Lord and my God!

Jesus, you are the Bread of Life. Thank you for sharing God's life with me. Help me to be true to you always.

Prayers After Communion

After we have received Jesus Christ, we should join in the communion song (page 29).

We remember that Jesus is with us. We can talk to him and tell him about our thanks, our needs, and our love. Here is a prayer you might also say.

> Jesus, you do such great things for me!
> You come to live within me.
> You fill me with your life.
> Help me to grow in loving you
> and in doing and being
> all that you wish.

Celebrating Reconciliation

How to Make Good and Loving Choices

1. Find a quiet "thinking" place to
   think about what you must do.

2. Pray:
   Holy Spirit, help me to make
   a good and loving choice.

3. Think about all the choices,
   good and bad, that you can make.

4. After thinking about each one, ask:
   If I do this, will it show that I love:
   - God?
   - others?
   - myself?

   If I say "Yes" to loving God
   and others and myself, it is a
   good choice.

5. Talk over all your choices with
   someone who can help you.

6. With God's help, choose to do
   the right and loving thing.

The Ten Commandments for Children

We show we love God when:

1. We think first of what God wants when we make choices.

2. We only use God's name with love and respect.

3. We keep Sunday as God's special day of prayer and rest.

We show we love ourselves and others when

4. We listen to and obey those who care for us.

5. We care for all living things and are peacemakers.

6. We care for our bodies and respect other

7. We do not take anything that is not ours.

8. We are truthful and fair to everyone.

9. We are faithful to those we love.

10. We help people to have what they need to live.

From Exodus 20:1–17

How to Examine Your Conscience

To examine your conscience, think
about the times you made an unloving
choice or chose to do what you knew
to be wrong. You sinned or disobeyed
God's Law on purpose.

To help you remember any time when
you may have made an unloving choice,
ask yourself questions like these:

1. When I make choices, do I sometimes
   forget to think first about what God wants
   me to do? Have I done what God wants?

2. Have I used God's name in a bad way?

3. Did I participate in Sunday Mass?

4. Have I disobeyed those who take care of me?

5. Have I given myself the good food
   and sleep my body needs?

6. Have I hurt someone by what I have
   said or done?

7. Have I taken money or anything that is not mine?

8. Have I always told the truth?

9. Have I been unfair to others—especially
   those who are different?

10. Have I refused to help needy people?

Making Up, or Reconciling

Think about how you will use your mouth or
your hands or your feet or your eyes or your
heart to make up, or reconcile, with those
you may have hurt by your unloving choices.

I Am
With You
Always

*Celebrating the
Sacrament of Reconciliation*

These things are always part of the celebration of the sacrament of Reconciliation.

- We examine our conscience and are sorry for our sins. We promise not to sin again.

- We confess our sins.

- We receive a penance.

- We pray an Act of Contrition.

- We receive absolution and thank God.

We can celebrate Reconciliation by ourselves with the priest or with others and the priest.

The priest greets me and reminds me
that God always loves me.

I make the sign of the cross.

He or I may read a story from the Bible.

I talk with the priest about myself.
I confess my sins: what I did wrong and why.
The priest talks to me about loving God
and others.
He gives me a penance.

I make an Act of Contrition. Here are two.*

1. My God,
    I am sorry for my sins with all my heart.
    In choosing to do wrong and failing
    to do good,I have sinned against you
    whom I should love above all things.
    I firmly intend, with your help,
    to do penance, to sin no more,
    and to avoid whatever leads me to sin.
    Our Savior Jesus Christ
    suffered and died for us.
    In his name, my God, have mercy.

2. Lord Jesus, Son of God,
    have mercy on me, a sinner.

*See page 46 for another Act of Contrition.

In the name of God and the Church,
the priest gives me absolution. (He may
extend or place his hands on my head.)
This means that my sins have been
forgiven and I answer:
    Amen.

The priest asks me to thank God for
God is good. I respond:
    His mercy endures forever.

The priest tells me to go in peace.

Celebrating the Sacrament with Others

We sing an opening hymn and the priest
greets us. The priest prays an opening prayer.

We listen to a reading from the Bible
and a homily.

We examine our conscience.
We make an Act of Contrition.

We may say a prayer or sing a song,
and then pray the Our Father.

We individually confess our sins to a priest.
In the name of God and the Christian community,
the priest gives us a penance and absolution.

Together we thank God for loving and forgiving us.

The priest blesses us, and we go in
the peace and joy of Christ.

My Reconciliation Song

1. Jesus you who blessed the children
   Bless me as I come to you.
   Bless my mouth to sing your praises
   For each day so fresh and new.
   Bless my hands to do your will and
   Comfort people weak and ill.
   Bless my feet to follow you and
   Walk your path so just and true.

2. Bless my ears that hear you tell me
   To be the best that I can be.
   Bless my eyes to see the beauty
   Of the love you have for me.
   Bless my heart to know your love and
   Feel your mercy from above.
   Bless my friends and family and
   Keep them safe and close to thee.
   Amen.

Music for this song can be found on
Sadlier's *With You Always: First Reconciliation* Video.

Our Catholic Prayers

Prayer is talking and listening to God. We can tell God what is in our hearts, using our own words, or we can say prayers that other Catholics pray.

There are many reasons why we pray:

- We pray to love and praise God.
- We pray to ask God's help.
- We pray to thank God for helping us.
- We pray to tell God that we are sorry for anything wrong we have done.

We can pray at any time. In the morning we can offer God all the things we will do that day. At night we can thank God for being with us all day.

God also wants us to pray as a parish community. We pray together when we celebrate Mass and the other sacraments.

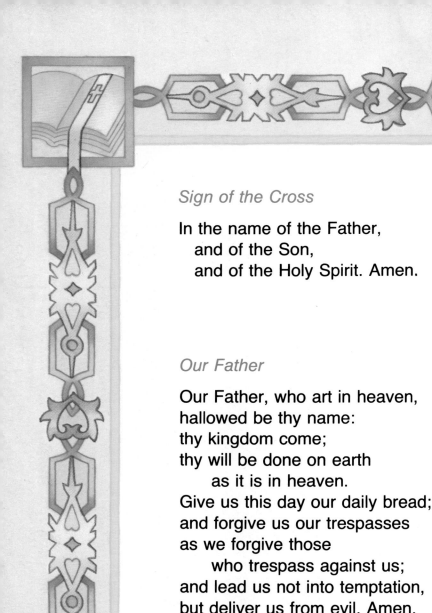

Sign of the Cross

In the name of the Father,
and of the Son,
and of the Holy Spirit. Amen.

Our Father

Our Father, who art in heaven,
hallowed be thy name:
thy kingdom come;
thy will be done on earth
as it is in heaven.
Give us this day our daily bread;
and forgive us our trespasses
as we forgive those
who trespass against us;
and lead us not into temptation,
but deliver us from evil. Amen.

Glory to the Father

Glory to the Father, and to the Son,
and to the Holy Spirit:
as it was in the beginning,
is now, and will be for ever. Amen.

Hail Mary

Hail Mary, full of grace,
the Lord is with you;
blessed are you among women,
and blessed is the fruit
of your womb, Jesus.
Holy Mary, Mother of God,
pray for us sinners now
and at the hour of our death. Amen.

An Act of Contrition

O my God, I am sorry for my sins.
In choosing to sin,
and failing to do good,
I have sinned against you
and your Church.
I firmly intend,
with the help of your Son,
to make up for my sins
and to love as I should.

The Angelus

The angel of the Lord
declared to Mary, and she
conceived by the Holy Spirit.
Hail Mary. . . .

Behold the handmaid of the Lord,
be it done to me according to your word.
Hail Mary. . . .

And the Word was made Flesh
and dwelled among us.
Hail Mary. . . .

Pray for us, O Holy Mother of God,
That we may be worthy of the
promises of Christ.

Let us pray:
Pour forth, we beseech you, O Lord,
your grace into our hearts that we to
whom the incarnation of Christ your Son
was made known by the message of
an angel may, by his passion and death,
be brought to the glory of his resurrection,
through Christ our Lord.
Amen.

These are prayers we can say before
and after meals to thank God for all
God's gifts.

Grace Before Meals

Bless us, O Lord,
and these your gifts
that we are about to receive
from your bounty,
through Christ our Lord. Amen.

Grace After Meals

We give you thanks, almighty God,
for these and all your gifts
that we have received through
Christ our Lord. Amen.

It is good to begin each day asking for God's help to live as friends of God.

Two Morning Offerings

1. My God, I offer you today
   All that I think and do and say,
   Uniting it with what was done
   On earth by Jesus Christ, your Son.

2. My God, I offer you all my prayers,
   works, and sufferings of this day
   for all the intentions of your most
   Sacred Heart. Amen.

We end our day giving thanks
for God's kindness and care for us.

An Evening Prayer

Dear God, before I fall asleep
I want to thank you for this day,
so full of your kindness and your love.
I close my eyes to rest now,
safe in your loving care.

The Apostles' Creed

I believe in God, the Father Almighty,
    creator of heaven and earth.

I believe in Jesus Christ,
        his only Son, our Lord.
    He was conceived by the power
            of the Holy Spirit
        and born of the Virgin Mary.
    He suffered under Pontius Pilate,
            was crucified, died, and was buried.
    He descended to the dead.
    On the third day he rose again.
    He ascended into heaven,
            and is seated at the right hand
                of the Father.
    He will come again to judge
            the living and the dead.

I believe in the Holy Spirit,
    the holy catholic Church,
    the communion of saints,
    the forgiveness of sins,
    the resurrection of the body,
    and the life everlasting. Amen.

Prayer for Someone Who Is Sick

Dear Jesus,

You touched and healed so many people when you were on earth.

Please now bring your healing love to

_____

who is sick.

Amen.

Prayer for Someone Who Has Died

Dear Jesus,

You told us that we will live forever in your love.

Take care of _____
and bring (him or her) to be
with you in peace and joy.

Amen.

Jesus,

You are my Good Shepherd.
Your love is all around me.
I trust that you will love
and care for me always.

Amen.

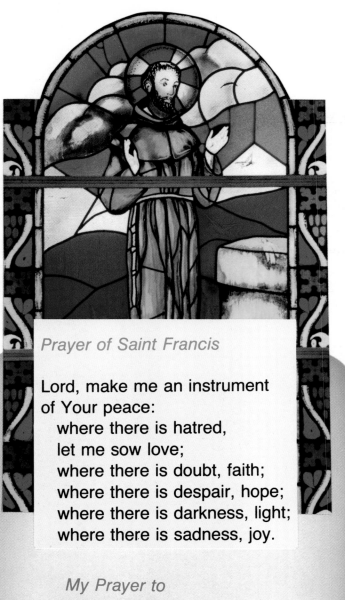

Prayer of Saint Francis

Lord, make me an instrument
of Your peace:
  where there is hatred,
  let me sow love;
  where there is doubt, faith;
  where there is despair, hope;
  where there is darkness, light;
  where there is sadness, joy.

My Prayer to
Be a Peacemaker

Dear God,

Please help me to be like
Saint Francis—one of your
reconcilers, one of your
peacemakers.

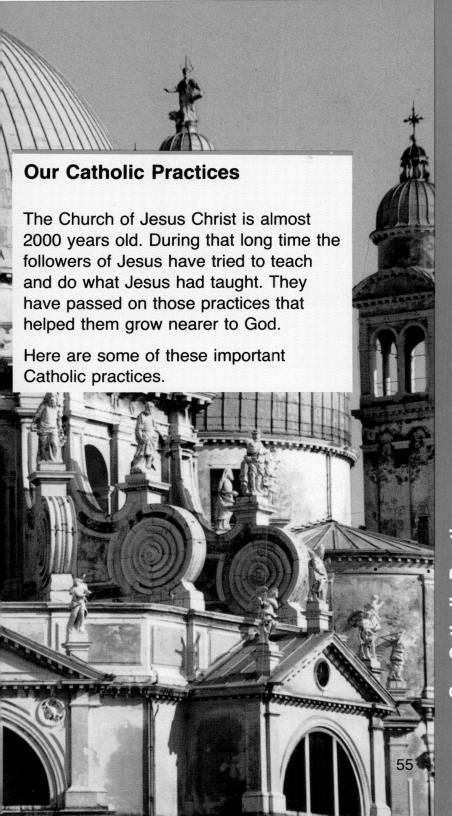

Our Catholic Practices

The Church of Jesus Christ is almost 2000 years old. During that long time the followers of Jesus have tried to teach and do what Jesus had taught. They have passed on those practices that helped them grow nearer to God.

Here are some of these important Catholic practices.

55

Near the end of Mass the priest places the remaining consecrated Bread in a special place called the tabernacle. The eucharist is kept there so that communion may be taken to people who cannot come to Mass.

When the eucharist is in the tabernacle, it is called the Blessed Sacrament. Many people come to church during the day to pray to Jesus. We call this practice making "a visit" to the Blessed Sacrament.

Benediction

At Benediction a large host, which was consecrated during Mass, is placed in a holder called a *monstrance* so that all can see the Blessed Sacrament. The priest lifts the monstrance and blesses the people with the sign of the cross.

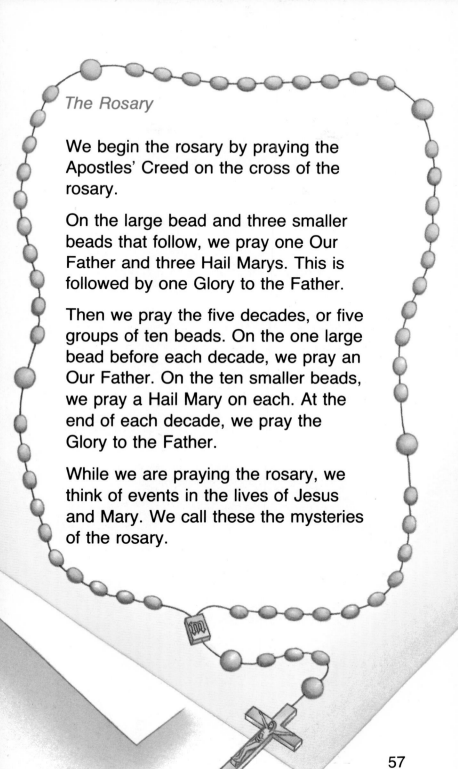

The Rosary

We begin the rosary by praying the Apostles' Creed on the cross of the rosary.

On the large bead and three smaller beads that follow, we pray one Our Father and three Hail Marys. This is followed by one Glory to the Father.

Then we pray the five decades, or five groups of ten beads. On the one large bead before each decade, we pray an Our Father. On the ten smaller beads, we pray a Hail Mary on each. At the end of each decade, we pray the Glory to the Father.

While we are praying the rosary, we think of events in the lives of Jesus and Mary. We call these the mysteries of the rosary.

As Catholics we look on our church as a very special place. We treat God's house with care and respect. In God's house we pray together as a parish family.

We genuflect toward the eucharist reserved in the tabernacle when we enter our pew in church. We stand, sit, and kneel at Mass as signs of respect.

Holy Things

Catholics use statues, medals, and paintings to help remind us of Jesus, Mary, and the saints. We never pray to these things but use them to help us think about God's love.

We also show respect for palms, ashes, candles, and anything we use in the celebration of our faith.

Blessings

We make the sign of the cross on ourselves with holy water to remind us of our Baptism.

As the priest blesses us during Mass and the sacraments, we make the sign of the cross.

The priest or deacon may bless statues, rosary beads, medals, and many other objects.

Parents may bless their children.

Blessing of Throats

Each year on February 3, the feast of Saint Blase, the Church blesses those who wish to pray for good health.

The priest, deacon, or other minister places two candles against the throat of each person and prays that the person will enjoy good health and be spared from diseases of the throat.

Lent is the forty days before Easter. It is a special time to show how much we love God, ourselves, and others.

The first day of Lent is called Ash Wednesday. On that day the priest places ashes on our forehead in the sign of the cross. He does this to remind us to try harder during Lent to live as Jesus asks us to live.

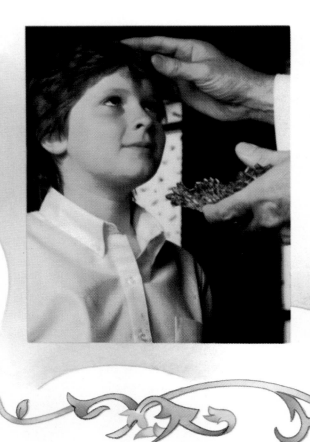

Holy Week begins on Passion, or Palm, Sunday. On this day we remember the day on which Jesus Christ rode into Jerusalem on a donkey and was greeted by the people with great joy. They broke off palm branches from the trees and waved them in the air, shouting:

"Hosanna to the Son of David! Blessed is he who comes in the name of the Lord!"

On this day the Church blesses palms as a part of the beginning of Mass. They are a reminder of Christ's entry into Jerusalem and that we should always welcome and reverence Christ who died for us.

The Way of the Cross (Stations)

In many of our churches we have beautiful reminders of what Jesus did for us on Good Friday. We call these the Stations of the Cross. Each station tells about one moment of Jesus' last journey before he died.

At each station we stop and think about how much Jesus loved us and what he did for us. Here is a prayer you can pray at each station.

Thank you, Jesus, for all you have done for us. We know that through your cross and resurrection you have saved the world.